Roberto Clemente

By Wil Mara

Consultant
Nanci R. Vargus, Ed.D.
Assistant Professor of Literacy
University of Indianapolis, Indianapolis, Indiana

Children's Press®
A Division of Scholastic Inc.
New York Toronto London Auckland Sydney
Mexico City New Delhi Hong Kong
Danbury, Connecticut

Designer: Herman Adler Design
Photo Researcher: Caroline Anderson
The photo on the cover shows Roberto Clemente.

Library of Congress Cataloging-in-Publication Data

Mara, Wil.
  Roberto Clemente / by Wil Mara.— 1st ed.
    p. cm.
  Includes index.
  ISBN 0-516-21845-X (lib. bdg.)   0-516-25824-9 (pbk.)
  1. Clemente, Roberto, 1934-1972—Juvenile literature. 2. Baseball players—
Puerto Rico—Biography—Juvenile literature. I. Title.
  GV865.C45M35 2005
  796.357'092—dc22

2004015311

CHILDREN'S PRESS, and ROOKIE BIOGRAPHIES®, and associated
logos are trademarks and or registered trademarks of Scholastic Library
Publishing. SCHOLASTIC and associated logos are trademarks and or
registered trademarks of Scholastic Inc.
1 2 3 4 5 6 7 8 9 10 R 14 13 12 11 10 09 08 07 06 05

Smack! Watch that ball go!

Do you like playing baseball?

Roberto Clemente did. He was
a great baseball player.

5

Clemente was born on August 18, 1934, in Puerto Rico.

When he was a child, Clemente loved sports. He liked baseball best.

In Puerto Rico, Clemente played ball with a club. Later, he joined a team called the Crabbers.

Then, he joined the Montreal Royals in Canada. Later, he went to the United States to play baseball.

Clemente is wearing his Crabbers uniform.

Clemente is wearing his Pirates uniform.

In 1954, the Pittsburgh Pirates asked Clemente to be on their team. Clemente said yes.

He played his first game in 1955. He was a Pittsburgh Pirate for 18 years.

Clemente was a great batter. He was voted the best batter in his league. Four times!

14

Clemente was also a great fielder.

He had a strong arm. He could throw the ball exactly where it needed to go.

There is a special award for great fielders. It is called the Gold Glove Award.

Clemente won the Gold Glove Award 12 times!

Clemente

This is Clemente receiving the Gold Glove Award.

This is Clemente playing in an All-Star Game.

18

There is a special game during each baseball season. It is called the All-Star Game.

The best players from one league play the best players from another league.

Clemente played in the All-Star Game 12 times!

Clemente helped the Pirates win two World Series.

He was voted the team's MVP in the second World Series. MVP stands for "Most Valuable Player."

Look at Clemente! He is on his way to home plate in this World Series game.

Clemente is practicing his swing.

On the last day of the 1972 season, Clemente made his 3,000th hit. Only ten other players had ever reached 3,000 hits.

Then, something terrible happened.

There was an earthquake in Nicaragua. Clemente wanted to help the people who were hurt.

He got on a plane that was going there. The plane was carrying food, clothing, and medicine.

Some buildings fell during the earthquake.

ROBERTO CLEMENTE WALKER
PITTSBURGH N. L. 1955–1972

MEMBER OF EXCLUSIVE 3,000-HIT CLUB. LED
NATIONAL LEAGUE IN BATTING FOUR TIMES. HAD
FOUR SEASONS WITH 200 OR MORE HITS WHILE
POSTING LIFETIME .317 AVERAGE AND 240 HOME
RUNS. WON MOST VALUABLE PLAYER AWARD 1966.
RIFLE-ARMED DEFENSIVE STAR SET N. L. MARK BY
PACING OUTFIELDERS IN ASSISTS FIVE YEARS.
BATTED .362 IN TWO WORLD SERIES, HITTING IN
ALL 14 GAMES.

The plane was very old. It caught on fire and crashed into the sea. Clemente died in the crash.

The next year, Clemente was voted into the National Baseball Hall of Fame.

If you go there, you will see this plaque. It will tell you about his baseball career.

Clemente is remembered as a great baseball player. He was also a great person.

You can see this statue of Clemente at Three Rivers Stadium in Pittsburgh, Pennsylvania.

29

Words You Know

All-Star Game

Crabbers uniform

earthquake

Gold Glove Award

Pirates uniform

Index

About the Author

More than fifty published books bear Wil Mara's name. He has written both fiction and nonfiction, for both children and adults. He lives with his family in northern New Jersey.

Photo Credits